The cat who wanted to fly high

(Journal Entries for April and May)

ENCHANTED MOUNTAIN

José Cañas Torregrosa

Illustrated by Mª Fe Quesada

The cat who wanted to fly high

(Journal Entries for April and May)

EVEREST

For Alberto and Elena
who –I know– also have
a raging desire
to fly into the future

Editorial Coordination: Ana María García Alonso
Layout: Cristina A. Rejas Manzanera

Original title: *El gato que quiso volar alto*
Translation by: Michael B. Miller

Cover Design: Jesús Cruz

Carretera León-La Coruña, km 5 - LEÓN
ISBN: 84-241-8045-3
Legal Registration: LE. 564-2001
Printed in Spain

EDITORIAL EVERGRÁFICAS, S. L.
Carretera León-La Coruña, km 5
LEÓN (España)

APRIL 12th

Floro gazes at the stork with so much envy! It is, however, an innocent kind of envy, nothing more than that. No one can say that Floro is an ambitious or egotistical cat, much less a violent and quarrelsome one. Rather he's just a very curious cat, and above all, shall I confess it now? He wants so badly to fly, to see things beyond the rooftops, to cast his eye down on the church bell tower, to do loops and swoops. He imagines the fresh air running through his whiskers, and the truly fantastic sensation of riding on a magic carpet of pink and white clouds. And what about the dark clouds? Floro doesn't like them at all because they're a sign of rain, and you must know that cats don't like water very much, even though rain is so clean, clear, and fresh.

The stork seems aware of Floro, as she likes to show off, flying and spreading her wings, acting like a majestic and powerful queen of the sky. Again and again she passes overhead, above Floro, who timidly meows each time and, with feline awe and meekness, keeps his eyes fixed on the bird's every loop.

Full of sighs, meows, and laments, Floro finally decides to come down from the church bell tower. He climbs with agility and care, moving cautiously along the rooftops of the town, making his way home to doña Paquita's house. Doña Paquita runs the only tobacco store in town, called simply "The Tobacco

Shoppe". And she is also Floro's guardian, his owner, his friend…

As he descends from the bell tower, Floro carries in his heart, a steady yearning to fly. He can picture himself with two wings, right in the middle of his back, two black and white wings, two wings that match the rest of his furry coat.

But his thoughts are interrupted by harsh reality. To get home, Floro must pass some very difficult obstacles: the uneven rooftops, set far apart, which drop dangerously in front of a balcony that he must reach, or risk falling on to a small patio, a patio with just a tiny space to land in. This leaves him feeling nervous, because even cats, while they're athletic and very agile, can have problems completing certain turns and leaps.

When this happens, when Floro is faced with a perilous obstacle, he concentrates and carefully calculates his leap. He must be brave and determined before he finally jumps and lands on his padded feet.

APRIL 12th

Doña Paquita unwraps the last shipment of Havana cigars that have arrived at The Tobacco Shoppe. She picks up the little wooden boxes of cigars, sniffs them one by one and cleans them with loving care, practically rocking them in her arms… Then, just as ceremoniously, she sets them out for display on the main shelf of her store for all to see.

When she finishes this little task, doña Paquita smiles and admires the cigars' plastic wrappers. They really are so nice, she thinks. She will sell these special cigars for weddings and fiestas, for celebrations with music and hand clapping, laughter and applause, coffee and cakes, shouts of "Long live the newly-weds" and "Long live the godparents, too. . . " You ought to know that in this little town, aside from the mayor and the pharmacist, no one smokes cigars except at weddings, baptisms, and the August Fair. Few people can afford to buy expensive cigars, fanciful things that go up in smoke and vanish in an instant.

At this point, and very confidentially, I'll tell you a well-guarded secret: doña Paquita doesn't smoke. She never has. In fact, she even hates tobacco. But no one knows that. Only Floro, who hears her talking to herself sometimes, unburdening her thoughts or praying to some saint or other, painfully and sincerely asking him for forgiveness. “But a person has to make a living somehow,” she always adds at the end of her prayer.

Despite these prayers, doña Paquita has never been too hard on herself or felt very guilty about her job. At the most, she just reads in an even tone, persuasively and with proper emphasis, that now familiar warning, “SMOKING CAN BE HAZARDOUS TO YOUR HEALTH”. She reads it to all the customers who buy a carton of cigarettes, especially to

adults who don't know how to read very well, and to young people who begin smoking because they think it makes them look older.

Gazing at her boxes of Cuban cigars, the cheerful and contented doña Paquita hears Floro's footsteps and purring. As soon as he arrives, Floro immediately begins rubbing his head and his back rhythmically against doña Paquita's legs, waiting for her to stroke him. And, as always, he gets what he wants.

"How's my favorite cat? Did you enjoy your walk?"

Naturally Floro doesn't reply, although he would be delighted if he could talk to doña Paquita, who is so full of kindness. Above all, he would love to share his secret with her, and simply tell her about his dreams of flying. This is why he blinks so sweetly as doña Paquita rubs him and whispers sweet things. Her buttery words must feel as soothing to Floro as the pampering touch of her hand.

APRIL 16th

Today's a good day for flying!" Floro thinks as he surveys the street from atop a balcony. It's a magnificent spring morning, and sunlight is just beginning to flood the streets with warmth.

Floro notices that doña Paquita has left home to open the tobacco shop. He's glad because he doesn't want anyone to witness his first attempt at flying.

And it isn't that he doesn't wish to share the possibility of his success with doña Paquita. It's that, at worst, he'll fail, and if he falls, he doesn't want his owner to feel sorry for him.

Stealthily Floro leaves the house through a trap door on the roof and scans the horizon, lifting his head and searching for the best place to make his first attempt at flying. He wiggles his ears like the antenna of some imaginary radar, looking past the rooftops to survey the scene before him.

"From the roof of that tall, abandoned house, the one with the peeling shingles! Without any humans around to see me, this ordeal will be much easier."

And he moves toward the house, proud and determined, ready to pass into history as the first flying cat.

Floro spends several hours observing the stork from the bell tower of the church. Unknowingly, she serves as an excellent instructor, flexing her feet, leaping into the air, and beating her wings. The result: a perfect take-off. And afterwards, high in the sky, she merely continues flapping her wings or takes advantage of the gusts of wind to glide, all the while enjoying the panorama and viewing the tiny dots below: the men and women, the houses, the church and the town, and everything else there is to see.

"I'm going to copy her, only I won't be flapping any wings, that's for sure! I'll have to flap my four paws just as hard as I can."

APRIL 16th

The journey to the abandoned house isn't too hard for Floro. It's one of frequent routes, since the house has sheltered several generations of cats that have raised families there for the past several years. People say that their owners had to emigrate a long time ago, to one of the cities in the north, far away. So the cats who live in that house honor the memories of their former owners, people who dreamed about a better future somewhere else. The cats are grateful to them for this house. So every day they fill the silence of that dwelling with their meows, big and small, an entire concert, so melodious that it sounds like a song in honor of those who left the cats to them. Here many generations of cats are born, raised, and grow up.

Floro's concerned if members of his own species are there to observe his first flight. Maybe he'll set an example for them, with his courage and daring. Perhaps the other cats will decide to imitate his example and a whole bunch of feline flocks will soon be sailing across the sky, high above the town.

Yes. No doubt about it! How great it would be to fly with Misifolio, the prissy little cat of don Ramón, the librarian, or with Bermenejo, the sacristan's favorite white cat… It would also be so nice to mew poems of love from above to Titilia, the lady pharmacist's cat;

Perhaps then, she'd stop being so aloof and elusive and bestow upon Floro, once and for all, a gaze sprinkled with a hundred romantic winks, one of those oh-so-pretty and very quick of which only cats are capable.

APRIL 16th

Floro finally makes his way to the abandoned house. He chooses the steepest eave, which faces what used to be a garden, where now only traces of it remain. Despite his excitement, he reaches the spot slowly and calmly, and he immediately glances down.

"This is pretty high! I've been here so many other times, but why does it seem much higher today than ever before?" Floro wonders.

Then he looks up, and what he sees seems a marvel to his eyes…

The sky is crystal clear, painted an intense and robust blue, almost electric in color. There isn't a cloud anywhere. But even higher than Floro is the stork; she seems to have chosen the church bell tower as her temporary but comfortable home for the past few days. "How nice of you, Señorita Stork, though it's your fault that I'm doing this!" Floro is undoubtedly thinking. "You've come to observe my first flight, haven't you? Well, just wait a moment; I won't disappoint you."

Then Floro looks down and sees five small cats looking up, watching him and his daring.

Our cat looks up at the sky again and, once more, finds himself gazing at the stork in flight. And so, four times, in what seems like a ceremony, Floro looks up and down, down and up: first at the sky, then at the earth. Either he'll know the glory of flying or the bitterness of the worst failure.

"Ready, set, go!" Floro says, and taking advantage of a soft breeze, he closes his eyes and leaps into the air. But just as soon as he jumps, he opens his eyes, because he doesn't want to

miss anything during his first flight. And he bats his paws in the air, all four of them, with all his might, with all…

But, oh, no! His weight betrays him, the law of gravity betrays him, reason betrays him, his heart and his very dreams betray him… and Floro falls, with a mighty plop, on top of a thick pile of leaves, before the astonished gazes of the little cats who are still shocked by his daring.

Floro is badly hurt. Fortunately the mound of leaves cushioned his fall. If it hadn't been for that, he could have been hopelessly smashed against the ground. He slowly utters a hollow meow of pain as he lies there, unable to move.

It often happens that fellowship among animals is greater than fellowship among humans. Soon the five cats, seeing Floro lying on the ground, rush to his aid. Two of them go off to look for help, while the rest lick the wounds of the injured cat in an effort to ease his pain.

APRIL 16th

We know what they say about "a cat having nine lives", but we also know that we don't know exactly what it means. Without that thick pile of leaves, and help from the cats from the abandoned house, Floro might not have survived his fall.

It was easy to identify Floro because of his little red collar, a gift from doña Paquita. Although parts of his body were numb and swollen from the fall, the little red collar with the golden bell told everyone that he belonged to the lady who ran The Tobacco Shoppe. These were the very same collar and the very same bell that Floro had fretted over because he didn't like any frills, and on more than one occasion, without doña Paquita knowing why, they had been the reason for his bad mood. But it was because of that collar that cat fellowship worked a miracle.

Floro, "the apprentice bird", was in terrible shape and had to be transported to doña Paquita's house with the greatest of care. Several cats picked him up gently in their mouths and carried him home.

This was the right decision, a decision made by the most experienced cat in the abandoned house. After listening for hours and hours to poor Floro's wailing, he saw that the poor cat could find no comfort, despite the tender care and attention of his fellow felines, which included the five witnesses to his short and disastrous little flight.

Thus, under the cover of night, a whole procession of cats takes the shortest route they know to doña Paquita's house.

Once there, they gently deposit poor Floro on doña Paquita's doorstep, and while the most experienced cat in the group knocks at the old, wooden door with his paws, accompanied by the rhythmic sound of his long, sharp nails, the rest of the cats meow the best of their repertoire in a mini-concert, which is soon interrupted when doña Paquita's neighbors turn on their outdoor lights and clear their throats. Doña Paquita's agitated neighbors hurl a cascade of shouts and even some shoes at the cats who have disturbed their sleep.

Then the cats take off running. Only the injured Floro is left behind, barely able to open his eyes when doña Paquita comes to the door.

"For goodness sake, Floro! What in the world happened to you? How did you do this to yourself?"

Of course, doña Paquita doesn't expect an answer, and she lovingly picks her cat up and puts him in the wicker basket that has been his home, his refuge, and his castle since he was born. She stays at Floro's side, administering iodine to his wounds and bandaging his limbs. She gives him lots of hugs and pampering, un til morning, when don Inocencio, the veterinarian, can come to examine him.

"Lord, Lord, what a mess this is! Give me the strength," doña Paquita repeats while watching over Floro, who begins to feel a little more cheerful and somewhat better, thanks to his owner's loving care.

APRIL 17th

There's no doubt about it. Floro is a lucky cat. Don Inocencio diagnoses him with multiple fractures and several bruises, but one thing is for sure: he'll live. That's for certain. The poor cat has no choice for now; he'll be confined to his basket for a long time. And so, Floro, although alive, looks like a little mummy, with his body in a cast from paw to paw. In the meantime, he's still very much resigned to his luck as a cat, having known both good and bad fortune, for you already know what they say about a cat having nine lives.

The days seem long to Floro, between his little bowls of fish soup and finely chopped sardines. His jaw hurts him so much he can barely eat, even though he's always been a big eater, up until the moment he tried to fly, that is! In the meantime, doña Paquita doubles her efforts and her pampering to help Floro get well as soon as he can.

Amid all the pampering and the special bowls of soup, she's in a dither, unable to explain any of this to herself.

"Who brought Floro to the front door? Who or what caused those bruises and injuries?" she wonders.

And all she knows is that the more she tries to find an answer to her questions, the more confused she feels, both in her head and in her heart. The questions get more muddled each time she tries to answer them, and they multiply themselves many times over into a big ball of doubts until she finally decides to stop thinking about them just so she can devote more time, if that's possible, to looking after her cat. She knows that Floro provides her with so much company and affection, two important and essential ingredients in facing the loneliness she feels ever since she lost her husband.

During this period of time, when doña Paquita has to give Floro extra attention, she serves her regular customers as quickly as she can when they come into her store to buy cigarettes or postage stamps[1]. The customers notice that she seems more serious than normal, and many young people miss her little lecture on TOBACCO and HEALTH.

"What's wrong with doña Paquita?" they ask each other. And immediately they have a thousand different thoughts about loneliness, and how it produces confusion in the minds of people, especially older ones, and about how being a widow has affected doña Paquita.

[1]*In Spain, the tabaquería or tobacco shop also sells postage stamps, postcards, and stationery.*

But doña Paquita is entirely totally unaware of what they're saying about her, for she only has time and energy for Floro who, day by day, to all outward appearances, is looking better even if, deep down in his feline heart, he still feels quite sad because he failed to make his magical dream of flying come true.

APRIL 24th

"I've got to face it. We weren't made to fly. It's not a question of agility but of wings and, possibly, weight… Probably, if I hadn't been eating so much those last few days. . ." Floro tells himself again and again. But, no! That's not the reason! Cats can't fly, that's all there is to it, because if they could, they would have done it a long time ago!

And the more he thinks about this, the further his thoughts carry him straight into the dark night of sadness.

In the meantime, doña Paquita doesn't know what to do with Floro. She talks to him all the time, pampers him, strokes him… even sings old lullabies to him as if her cat were a real baby, and she does it with the greatest enthusiasm, even if the words are a bit silly:

“This good cat
who was born at night
wants to be taken out
for a ride in the car.

If my good cat
should soon drift off to sleep
I'll give him
sardines, perhaps,
and if he should wake up,
if he opens his little eyes,
then I'll take away his sardines
one by one.

A na, na, na, na…

This pretty, little cat
who was born at night
wants to go out for a ride
in the car.

The car isn't running and needs to be fixed,
the poor driver has one bad arm,
and the colts
will soon be running through the field.

This good cat
wants to fall asleep
with one eye open…
April's already gone."

What a silly lullaby! But I must tell you that doña Paquita's newfound fondness for singing lullabies is yet another strange thing that her neighbors have noticed of late.

Incidentally, the truth is that the good woman doesn't carry a tune very well. Floro who puts on a painful face of feline resignation isn't the only one whose ears suffer from doña Paquita's singing, for the ears of her neighbors suffer as well.

That is why the neighbors have joined in a chorus of daily gossip, commenting on doña Paquita's mania for singing lullabies to her cat and changing the words to make them suitable to Floro's liking, lullabies that her own parents must have sung to her many, many years ago, when she herself, unimaginable as this may seem, was quite little and beginning to learn about the world.

APRIL 28th

Neither lullabies nor pampering, neither fish soup nor a plate of chopped sardines satisfies Floro. He just stares out the window, looking ever so sad. It seems all that exists in his world is the window and what lies beyond it: the birds swaying happily on the branches of the trees in a springtime that seems to last forever. Doña Paquita is at a loss to lift his spirits. Nothing is working, not even the colorful wool threads or the toy mice he liked to play with as a kitten.

All that exists for Floro are the window and the universe beyond it, a universe in motion, in clear contrast to his situation, stuck inside a cast, stuck in his basket, and none of it by choice.

It's also very hot. This is why doña Paquita decides to throw open the window.

And that's the moment Floro ought to seize, to stretch his neck and try to see beyond the windowpanes. Still weak and sore, he tries the best he can, but he's in pain, and it's not worth the effort.

"Oh, my poor little Floro, you're feeling hot, too," doña Paquita tells him. "I'll just set you down next to the window. The air will do us both some good,"

And there, by the window, Floro sees the stork again, the silent witness to his dream, fluttering her wings in the sky, and who knows?… maybe she's looking for him. At this moment, Floro's eyes are fixed on her and nothing else. Those big, almond-shaped, piercing eyes of his peer out, and Floro follows the stork's every move the best he can, his honeylike eyes going round and round in a waltz of wild spins. What does he see? He sees a love letter suspended in the sky, a kite that's floating free, a question mark that sways in the clouds, a floating heart, a song in flight, a caress, a poem in motion.

For the first time, doña Paquita notices Floro's fascination with the stork. She sees his little feline head following the bird and the fluttering of her wings. Doña Paquita is an observant woman, and for her this is a clear sign of Floro's interest in the bird.

So she conducts an experiment. She takes Floro's basket and moves it away from the

window for a moment. And immediately Floro begins to protest, meowing desperately.

"All right, all right… I'm sorry, dear friend. I wanted to see something. See now? I'm putting you back where you were."

Floro, still feeling desperate, anxiously searches the sky for the stork, and after a few seconds he again spots her. Once more, his eyes and the rest of his senses are focused only on her, once more with the same sweet, innocent fascination.

MAY 5th

It's not just the question of a single day. Many days have passed, and it's always the same thing. Sometimes doña Paquita takes Floro up to the rooftop still in his cast, still unable to move and the whole business repeats itself. Meanwhile, other birds arrive, but it's obviously the stork that Floro feels most drawn to. That's what doña Paquita concludes after many days of careful observation. And you know very well that she's right.

Floro has improved quite a bit, but he's still confined to his little basket, which has almost become a part of him, an extended part of his paws and his crippled body. He's like a creative living insidc a snail shcll.

Doña Paquita moves the little basket around the house so that while Floro is convalescing, he won't always feel so confined. But he continues to prefer the rooftop or the windowsill, especially during the day, when the birds are flying around. At night he sleeps nearly nonstop, probably remembering the time when he was a little kitten, a new feline on the block, because you can see him twitching nervously in his basket, but basically he appears to be smiling and seems happy in his dreams.

One morning, Floro finds himself a little better, and is no longer content to just follow the flight of the stork. It's clear and doña Paquita notices that he's eager to leave his little basket, which must feel like a prison to him by now, because Floro is arching his back, and it appears that he's ready to get up any minute, to pounce once more on some object he has in his sights, the way things were before the "accident".

The townspeople, while appearing less disturbed about things since doña Paquita has stopped her singing, haven't stopped commenting on the latest development: The Tobacco Shoppe is closed most of the time.

Because of her sudden decision to only open the store once in a while, many of her customers have had to buy their cigarettes down at Genaro's Tavern. And the truth is that her customers appear quite upset, because they say that their cigarettes cost more at Genaro's. What's more, they say, their letters are not being mailed on time, which is another function of The Tobacco Shoppe. During this period, with doña Paquita spending all of her time, especially the mornings, looking after Floro, it's been difficult to buy postage stamps since the store is rarely open for business.

I want to tell you that because of this, there is now a citizens' protest, growing bigger by the day, with people talking at great length about the happenings that have been affecting doña Paquita of late. And the fact is that the poor woman hasn't hurt anyone; in fact, they can't hold anything against hcr. Shc's always been friendly and affectionate to everybody who comes into her store.

But I don't want to keep anything from you. There are some very angry people in the town, and among them, the hardcore smokers have it in for her the worst of all. Some of them can be found on any street corner, or at the Workers and Artisans Club, and in the Central Plaza there are yet other groups, smaller ones, and many doubts have arisen among them, to the point where ill winds have begun to blow.

Doña Paquita doesn't know it yet, but a committee of neighbors in the town has already gone to see the mayor, to lodge their complaints.

"You've got to do something, Gervasio. We can't allow The Tobacco Shoppe to be closed all the time. It would be easy enough to turn

the concession over to someone else. If doña Paquita can't run it properly, somebody else here would be very happy to take over such a prosperous little business, one that's very important for the majority of townspeople," says don Ricardo, a local cattle breeder and a rich man, emphatically stating his case.

And so, Don Gervasio, the mayor, has heard their complaints.

"It's a pity," he says. "You all know quite well that Nicolás, her husband, was a close friend of mine and, above all, a very fine per-

son. The City Council did the right thing at the time, in supporting doña Paquita's application for a business license for the tobacco shop. It would be a sad and nasty trick to take it away from her now."

"But she already receives a very nice widow's pension," the cattle breeder asserts. "She won't starve. The Tobacco Shoppe ought to be handed over to someone else, above all to a person with a better head for business."

"What are you insinuating, don Ricardo?" the mayor asks, sounding quite serious.

"Just this," he tells the mayor, "and you know it as well as anyone here, that doña Paquita has gone off her rocker, that she's been a little unbalanced for some time now… In other words, and let me be clear about it: she's NUTS! And we've got to do something. As far as the rest of us are concerned, it can't go on like this any longer."

The rest of the members of the committee support everything that don Ricardo has said, in no uncertain terms, while the mayor, don Gervasio, is left feeling very sad as he mulls over the comments he's just listened to, in his office.

MAY 6th

Floro continues to improve but he's still confined to his basket, his own little throne, as it were… And it's obvious that he also continues watching the stork as she swoops through the sky, flying back and forth, though less frequently now, above the town, and what's more, summer is coming on. But the times that Floro has seen her majestically flapping her wings are quite rare of late. That's why, when today at noon, the stork appeared above the rooftop, Floro surely experienced a special feeling, something that doña Paquita noticed right away.

"Well, look who came to say hello to you," she says, sounding very sure of herself.

And so Floro tries once more, though unsuccessfully, to climb out of his wicker basket. The poor cat feels so desperate that he mews dejectedly.

"But, what's the matter?" doña Paquita asks him.

Floro looks at her first and then at the stork, and several more times in what appears to be an extraordinary effort to say something.

"No, it can't be! It's not possible. I must be going crazy, but… it seems to me that you… No, it can't be!" doña Paquita babbles.

Floro doesn't take his eyes off her. The poor woman refuses to believe the animal's fall had something to do with his fascination with the stork. But finally she understands. The evidence is clear, even if it's only a hint. Now it all seems so logical…

"So, that's what happened; you jumped at the stork and you fell into space… or maybe… you wanted… to fly. What am I talking about? Oh, Nicolás, help me. I can't solve this whole mess by myself!"

Doña Paquita, as you see, is talking to herself, caught in a sea of confusion. She knows that something out of the ordinary must have happened.

"And so you want to fly, is that it? How can I help you?" she asks, her head now ready to explode with the very idea of it. Without knowing exactly what she's looking for, doña Paquita searches all the drawers, closets, and cupboards in her house, until she finally spots something, and that something puts an end to what she's looking for. It's a plastic bag filled with all kinds of balloons of all different colors, and just waiting for somebody to blow them up.

"Suppose I blow these balloons up and tie them to his basket? But wait, that's not possible; the balloons won't lift the basket and I don't have enough air in my lungs to do the job. Anybody knows that," doña Paquita reasons. "I'd have to use the kind of gas they use at the carnivals to blow up the balloons. But what kind of gas do they use for that?"

Now, as you see, she's getting into something she doesn't know anything about. Her eyes survey the entire house, looking for an answer. Here and there and everywhere, including the adjacent office and The Tobacco Shoppe. Doña Paquita's eyes carefully search every corner of her house.

Finally she thinks of a possible solution: cigarette smoke. Why not give it a try?

And so doña Paquita prepares to light her first cigarette. She takes a balloon in her right

hand and then takes a big puff on the cigarette, and then, just before she starts coughing like crazy, she quickly releases all the smoke into the neck of the balloon.

It takes her a while to fill her first balloon, but it's not a very good solution, because the balloon won't stay up. Doña Paquita begins to feel defeated, and lowers her eyes… Fortunately, she's not one to give up very easily. She decides to look for a different solution.

And that's when her eyes fall on the little boxes of Havana cigars she so carefully guards in her store.

"Would the smoke from the Havanas work better?" she asks herself, and immediately she

picks up one of those little boxes, opens it and lights a cigar, and oh, what a fine aroma it has!

It's almost the same thing she did moments ago with the cigarette, except that now it takes more effort, but at last, to her satisfaction, she has proved her idea. The balloon stays up, wanting to escape into the sky, the aroma of the Cuban cigar trapped inside the little red sphere.

"This is going to work. Only now, I'll probably need more balloons, all the ones in this bag. And I don't know how long it will take me," doña Paquita says, very proud of herself and her experiment, but deeply worried about the amount of work involved. All that puffing, all that blowing.

MAY 11th

Many townspeople have seen her smoking for days on end, one cigar after another, as she goes on inflating all those colorful balloons. “Doña Paquita definitely isn’t right in the head,” the neighbors say.

In the meantime, she has been storing all the balloons in a room in her house, waiting for the right moment to tie them to Floro’s basket.

And that moment comes on a clear afternoon. So, once more she goes to the rooftop, the most natural place to carry out her idea. Today the sun gently warms the roofs of the houses. It's not too hot, and the stork is flying around again like the queen of the sky, her own private domain.

Doña Paquita ceremoniously carries Floro up to the roof in his basket, just so he can see the stork, and as usual his gray eyes are fixed on his owner's face, looking for an answer. And doña Paquita, just as ceremoniously, ties the balloons (now pointing skyward) to the basket, one by one, creating a whole symphony of colors around the wicker basket. And she would have finished attaching all of them if someone

hadn't knocked so hard and furiously at her door. Doña Paquita stops what she's doing and tenderly pats Floro's little head, her would-be-winged Icarus.

"I'm coming, I'm coming!" she calls, hurrying downstairs to answer the door, with all that loud knocking. Upon opening it, she sees Rafael, the town policeman, standing there.

"What in the world, Rafael, what's so urgent?" she asks.

"I'm sorry, doña Paquita, but I thought that if you were upstairs, you wouldn't hear me knocking," Rafael tells her.

"Well, what is it that brings you here with so much urgency?"

"An official notice from the Office of the Mayor", he says, handing her the papers. "They told me it was very urgent. That's the reason I rushed," Rafael adds, trying to make an excuse for himself.

Doña Paquita puts on her black-rimmed glasses, the ones she has hanging around her neck on a cord of the same color, and immediately begins reading the notice aloud, without paying much attention to Rafael's presence:

"In view of the fact that the establishment known as The Tobacco Shoppe, run by doña Francisca Morales de la Fuente, has remained closed an unusual and unacceptable amount of time, without the knowledge of the Mayor's Office, and consequently, without the explicit permission of the Municipal Government, the City Council, having met in full session on urgent business, has resolved the following:

To close said establishment, considered to be a public utility and of primary necessity (it being the only one of its kind in the city), and cancel (as stipulated in the contract under which it was opened) the license of said place of business, and transfer its operation to Don Joaquín Ramírez…"

She didn't bother to finish reading it. Doña Paquita seemed somewhat perturbed at first, but she very quickly recovered her composure. She still had enough strength and spirit to smile and dismiss Rafael, the City Council's official messenger, who had been standing there, studying the woman's face for a reaction. Instead, doña Paquita merely closed the door and, as she walked upstairs, she quickly thought back over all the years she had spent behind the counter of The Tobacco Shoppe, selling cigarettes and boxes of cigars and postage stamps to the people of her town. She had the feeling that it had all been a dream, a kind of magic show that had been conducted under the lens of a high-speed camera, but then the image of her husband immediately came to mind to comfort her. She wouldn't suffer financially because her widow's pension was enough to take care of her most urgent needs. And what's more, she had Floro.

"Oh, my goodness!" she thought. "Poor Floro's still up there, waiting for me!"

MAY 11th

Doña Paquita runs up the stairs in leaps and bounds, and hurrying, reaches Floro. Once she sees him, she calms down. There he is, inside his little basket of balloons, a little basket that's straining to take off from the rooftop and fly.

Doña Paquita resumes the job she started earlier and continues tying more and more balloons to the little basket. Floro's not only watching the stork but Doña Paquita, too, and

he's growing more nervous and excited the whole time. He senses how the little basket seems to want to fly away with him every time doña Paquita attaches another balloon. And he grows more and more excited, because he has an idea of what is about to happen.

A pair of strong cords holds the little basket in place on the roof and keeps it from shifting around.

"What's going to happen when I attach this blue balloon, the last one, and cut the cords to the basket?" doña Paquita wonders. "My goodness, how exciting this is!" she tells herself.

It seems that the stork is watching all of this, not wanting to miss anything. There she is, showing off like she always does, like a queen with wings.

Doña Paquita prepares to cut the cords. Her right hand, the one holding the scissors, is trembling. Before she does anything though, she seems to make the sign of the cross, or at least something like that, calling upon some divine power to help her in her mission.

When she finally does cut the first cord, the little basket tips and is pulled upwards on one side. Doña Paquita thinks it's going to work. Big tears fill the eyes of this good woman, who wants to make her cat happy, a cat who dreams about flying...

When she cuts the second cord, the little basket rights itself and levels off. More and more tears bathe doña Paquita's eyes because the little basket, now looking like a ball of light with all those colorful balloons, and challenging all logic and reason, rises higher and higher, and inside, there's Floro, looking so perplexed, his eyes turning every which way.

"Oh, my dear little friend, bon voyage! See you soon... But fly now... Fly as high as you can. And say hello for me to the stork and all the birds that cross your path for me, and if you should happen to see my husband's spirit while you're up there, please tell him not to despair, that it won't be long before we see each other again!"

And while doña Paquita is shouting and waving, filled with emotion and happiness, the townspeople gather and witness with amazement that extraordinary sight. And in the crowd of people, one sees the delighted faces of little boys and girls, and also the faces of a few insensitive adults who are laughing crudely and cruelly. And the only thing the townspeople see in the sky holds their undivided attention: a wicker basket pulled along by an array of colorful balloons, a light little basket, and inside, a cat greeting a perplexed stork with his feline meows, a cat offering from way up in the sky a serenade of gratitude to the woman who, down there, in her veil of tears, is wildly waving at him like a little bird flapping its wings, when all his heart is fluttering with joy.

CONTENTS